AN ANTHOLOGY OF POETRY

Wild

Hey
Hey
BOOKS

AN ANTHOLOGY OF POETRY

Contents

Contest Winners

Wild

AN ANTHOLOGY OF POETRY

Marcie Flinchum Atkins

About the Contributor

Marcie Flinchum Atkins is a teacher-librarian by day and a children's book writer in the wee hours of the morning. She holds an M.A. and M.F.A. in Children's Literature from Hollins University. She is the author of several nonfiction books, including *Wait, Rest, Pause: Dormancy in Nature* (Millbrook Press, 2019). Marcie's poetry for children has also been featured in several anthologies. For more information about Marcie's books and poetry, visit her at www.marcieatkins.com and on Twitter and Instagram @marciefatkins.

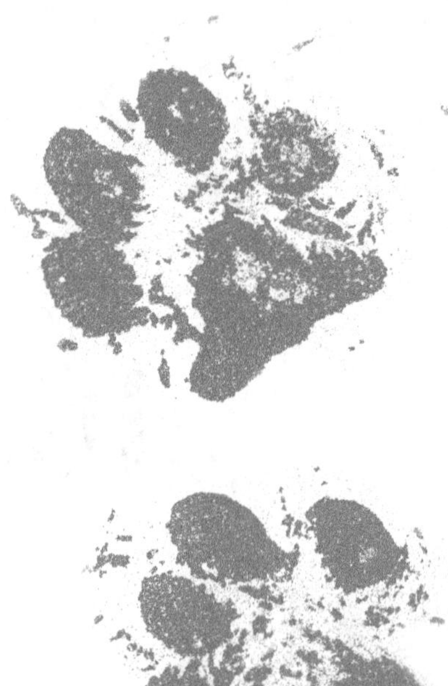

Untitled

out of tree crumbs
tiny mushrooms stake
their umbrellas

The Silence of Wildflowers

They don't burst in with "SURPRISE"
or twirl their colorful frocks.

They don't megaphone the bees
or beg for sun's spotlight.

They don't whistle for the wind to dance
or screech at tiny sniffers who pluck them.

They don't announce the dawn like the birds
or pass out sneezes to people like trees.

The wildflowers sneak up out of the ground
in silence.

An Apology to Poetry: Ars Poetica

I usually find you in the fuzz
of a dead bee
or the raindrop lingering on a leaf.

Sometimes you sneak into the creek
where the water striders skate
and the tulip poplar blooms are laid to rest.

You might sweep across the sky
like a watercolor brush
or in the darkening of dusk.

Often you twirl
in the cotton candy clouds of dawn,
sing with the sunrise birds.

It's not that you're hiding—
you're there.
Waiting to be noticed.

I fear I have ignored you
while staring at a screen
instead of scanning the sky.

I know I have rushed
past you in a parking lot
instead of looking down at the ant line.

Forgive me
for not noticing
when you wave.

Untitled

in a damp forest
lichen drips from the branches—
pale jewelry of trees

Benjamin Bishop

About the Contributor

Benjamin Bishop is a married father of three children and resides in Southern California, where he enjoys the beach and camping.

Benjamin teaches English Language Arts and has both a Bachelors and Masters in English Literature.

Benjamin was co-winner of the 2023 haiku contest on TheHumanist.com. He also has fiction and poetry published in Clever Fox Literary Magazine and is currently working on his upcoming poetry collection, *A Ballad of Yesterday and Tomorrow*.

Flowers in a Meadow

Life is a magical meadow of mistakes.
Sweet ambrosia nectar
Cultivated for but a hurried season in time.
Briefly twirling with sun-glazed tulips,
Dancing with star-speckled daffodils,
All whilst cradling colors of waning sunsets.
Drifting away like petals on a cool breeze,
Sprinkling a trail of golden pollen,
Leaving memories across the sky.

The Willow Tree

Strawberry spring
Under our willow tree
Morning fog settles
Hiding memories
Of immortal love
Weeping for loves lost
Etched on a tattooed tree
Scratched out
And forgotten
Incomplete dreams.

The Waiting Bench

I sit on the sturdy bench and I wait, watching
As the dandelions begin to sprout up and around
My feet and the sparrow eggs begin to hatch.
A butterfly flutters passed my ear, landing on
A blade of grass as a soft rain begins to spatter
My face, making small puddles. The tears
Come and I stand and splash my feet.

The bench has begun to splinter and crack.
I watch and wait as a bee buzzes and lands on
A sunflower, swaying in the sunshine. A warm
Breeze carries the sweet aroma of a crackling
Oak fire as an eagle circles in the clouds above,
Making small cries. I weep below,
Pacing around the bench.

The bench is now chipped and scratched and I
Watch and wait as the pieces fall like the orange
And yellow leaves, slowly drifting through the air.
A squirrel runs back and forth gathering brown
Acorns and a plump green apple falls to the ground.
A crisp, cool fog slowly settles on the ground,
Making a small, light mist. I sit and breathe in.

The bench is now broken and decayed, but I still
Watch and wait as snowflakes dance around me,
Coming to rest on the pine needles of a fir tree.
A white bunny picks at the shrubs, looking for
Red berries and a cardinal rests on a pine cone.
A cold gust of wind passes by, making a small
Blizzard around me. I close my eyes and exhale.

Candice Marley Conner

About the Contributor

Candice Marley Conner is the kidlit haint at a haunted indie bookstore, a Local Liaison for SCBWI, and an officer for her local writer's guild. Her short stories and poems are in various anthologies and magazines including *Woolgathering, Highlights Hello, Cabinet of Curiosities, Babybug,* and *Chicken Soup for the Soul*. She is the author of picture books: M IS FOR MOON PIE, CHOMPSEY CHOMPS BOOKS and SASSAFRAS AND HER TEENY TINY TAIL, and the YA Southern mystery, THE EXISTENCE OF BEA PEARL. She lives in Alabama with her husband and two children (one of whom is possibly feral and definitely a velociraptor.)

Candice is represented by Katelyn Detweiler at Jill Grinberg Literary Management.

Haiku of Morning, Noon and Night

Early sunshine hangs
rainbows on dragonfly wings.
Mouse squeaks welcome day.

The red snapdragon
growls at the chirping cricket,
No one can hear me!

Moon's turn to shine as
sun sleeps—pink to inky sky.
Stars streak wild with joy.

When I Am Among the Big Leaf Magnolia (A Mary Oliver inspired poem)

When I am among the trees,
especially the willow oak and the big leaf magnolia,
way back when and now and again exist therein.
Watch.

A Carolina wren egg cracks open,
ancient and dinosaur-like in its grace.
A moth supper is served.
Rain falls.
Clouds scurry across the sky
the small brown bird chased the moth through.
Flight wings out
downy feathers sprout.

The person I was as a child
watches wide-eyed in wonder
along with the person I am at this moment in time,
the person I will be tomorrow
and again,

all when I am among the willow oak
and big leaf magnolia.

With The Bees

We hummed with the bees today.
Our cupped hands filling, saying
Look! Here! Oh treasures!
Broken
curling snake egg shells,
hard bits of amber
from the pine
that got struck
by lightning
last summer.

We picnicked with the bees today.
Sipping on honeysuckle
our straws stamens, our cups
fuzzy
against
lips.

With the bees, we tucked mimosa
blooms in our hair
that tangled
when we turned
thankful for it.
Thankful for the day.
Thankful
for the wild hum
around us.

Patricia Cooley

About the Contributor

Patricia Cooley is an author, educator, and storyteller. She has taught reading and writing with K-8 students for over 30 years. She holds a Professional Educational License with endorsements in elementary education, secondary education, administration, gifted education, Spanish, English, and Language Arts.

She has studied poetry and writing at the Institute of Children's Literature, Society for Children's Book Writers and Illustrators, Lyrical Language Lab, 12 X 12 Book Challenge, Highlights Foundation, Children's Book Insider, Pomelo classes, the ABCs of Poetry, and ongoing conferences.

Patricia's publications include:

And the Crowd Goes Wild; A Global Anthology of Sports Poems

Highlights Hello, High Five, and High Five Bilingue Magazines

Teacher in Focus

Stories for Children

Owl Sees All

Scoping the forest
with binocular vision,
owl misses nothing.

Mountain vs. Ant Hill

Mountain
rocky, steep
hiking, climbing, rappelling
cliffs, peak, mound, holes
tunneling, nesting, emerging
dirty, low
Ant Hill

Linda M. Crate

About the Contributor

Linda M. Crate (she/her) is a Pennsylvanian writer whose poetry, short stories, articles, and reviews have been published in a myriad of magazines both online and in print. She has twelve published chapbooks, the latest being Searching Stained Glass Windows For An Answer (Alien Buddha Publishing, December 2022). She is also the author of the novella Mates (Alien Buddha Publishing, March 2022). Her debut book of photography, *Songs of the Creek* (Alien Buddha Publishing, April 2023), was recently published.

so much green

nature is resilient
and wise,
she does not need us
yet she has always
been kind to me;

perhaps she recognizes
the wilds in me that they
are always trying to tame or
tell me to swallow down—

i hear the music in the wings
of honey and bumble bees,
feel the compassion of trees,
appreciate the wings of birds in
flight;

once a majestic crow
welcomed me into the forest
and you cannot convince me
there is not magic in a place
where there is so much life and
so much green.

ocean visit

the ocean
danced a different blue
than the horizon,
yet i couldn't tell where
one ended and the other
began;

every time i visit the ocean
her roars calm the monsters
of my mind and her waves wash
away the things i no longer need
to carry—

little crabs run across the sand
beneath the moon in the dark,
and we catch them and then release
them;

there are living sand dollars
near the shore—

we saw the huge broken shell
of a horse shoe crab on the
sand one morning, and i wondered
what predator got to it.

outsiders

sea turtles
are my favorite
ocean creature

even if you aren't allowed
to touch them,
i don't mind simply observing
them because they are
beautiful;

i heard someone say they're mean—

but maybe that's the price
they have to pay to live in the ocean,
if you aren't aggressive then you
might get eaten by the creatures that
live in the depths;

and i don't think it's fair to say
they're mean even if they don't like humans—

we don't like people invading our
homes,
and they probably view us as
outsiders.

coffin for the living

i saw a pronghorn
antelope for the first time
when my family made
a trip to north dakota to
see my uncle and his new wife,
and i will never forget
the beauty and majesty in a
creature so wild and free
simply existing and being;
they watched our car
as it drove past:
unbothered—
simply curious and ever watching
before they disappeared into
the multi-colored sculpture of land
behind them in it's various reds
and browns,
it made me think perhaps animals are
the free ones and we're the one caged;
because what is a house but a
coffin for the living?

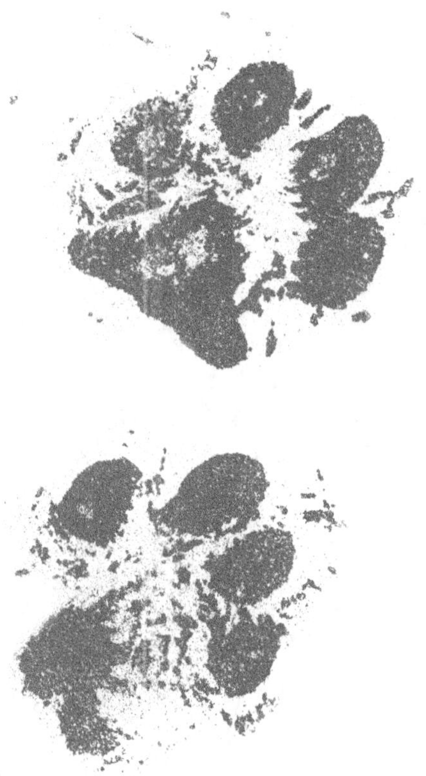

Robert Daniel

About the Contributor

Robert Daniel lives in Alabama and spends most of his time working as an engineer and providing for his wife and kids. When he's not working, he's busy on the homestead, rarely on social media, and trying to keep his kids off the phone, too. He has only just started pursuing a life-long passion for writing. *Fly* and *Wild* are his first poetry publications.

dinner with the family

every friday evening on my way home from work,
i stop to fill up at the little gas station outside of town.
there's really nothing else around except some trees
i just pump gas into my truck and watch the sun
sink into the ground. usually, i'm the only one
here, me and the cashier, but then little beady eyes
glow from the bushes and trees. and into the light
of the gas station, a family of raccoons come and sit, waiting.
i go inside the store and purchase some beef jerky, i
don't know if they should be eating the stuff, but
they don't seem to mind. tearing a few pieces off,
i toss the meat on the ground and then eat the rest.
that'll be the only family meal i share tonight. by the
time i get home, my kid will be asleep and my wife
would have already put dinner in the fridge. she would
have left me a plate on the table, just far enough from
the edge that the dog couldn't reach it, but the food
will be cold, and i'll have to heat it up in the microwave.
getting back in my truck, i pull out of the parking lot
and in my rearview mirror, i see the bushy tails
of the raccoons disappearing back into the dark brush.

the celebrity

amid the great smoky mountains,
the car inches forward,
stopped by the taillights in front
and those in front of that one.
thirty minutes of bumper to bumper.
no houses, no general stores, no traffic lights.
i come upon the scene for all this dismay.
high in the jaded canopies, a dark shape.
drivers slow so that passengers
can roll down their windows.
people pull over to get out
of their cars and stare up.
strangers take pictures and point,
talking in hushed tones.
the bear lays idly in the tree,
legs dangling on either side.
he yawns and rests
his head on the branch.

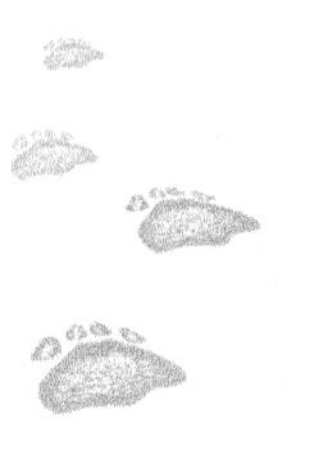

a hike

thick socks and ankle high boots
a camelbak less full of water
than when i started
fifteen miles from the parking lot
the trail—seldom used has overgrown
passing vines and bushes, branches
that grasp my pant legs as if
wanting me to stay
i do, how could i not
stay for the rest of the afternoon
sweat stained shirt
and stomach craving a burger,
i step out onto the pavement,
the world different from before
behind me, the wind rustles the leaves
woodsy hands waving adieu

it's just a road

<table>
<tr><td>

wild trees grow throughout
nothing stands in their wa
foothills and even claim bo
the other day. like a need
it stood straight up, out o
woodlands, but with a flaw.
only area where light touch
the tar-colored scar with
dashes. it breaks the forest i

</td><td>

the rolling mountains.
y. they take root in the
ulders. i saw one
le in a pin cushion,
f the rock. such mighty
its only weakness, the
es the forest floor, is its scar.
yellow ribbons and white
n two. unnatural.

</td></tr>
</table>

Leslie Degnan

About the Contributor

Leslie Degnan is a former teacher who writes picture books and poems for children. Her poems have been published in anthologies such as *What is Family?(2023)* and *Hop To It: Poems to Get You Moving (2020)*. When she's not writing, you'll find her outdoors birdwatching from her kayak or listening to birdsong in the meadow. You can find her on Twitter @DegnanLeslie.

CAROLINA WREN (WC:36)

"Tea-kettle, tea-kettle, tea!"
Calls the Carolina Wren.

Reminds me of a rooster's crow,
Again, again, and again.

Wren perches on a high tree branch,
And throws back his little head,

"Tea-kettle, tea-kettle, tea!"
Calls the Carolina Wren.

REDWING MEANS SPRING (WC:42)

The cattail marsh is silent and cold.
Ice thaws. Snow melts.
The marsh takes on an earthy scent.

On a chilly spring wind, redwings return,
Puffed up black feathers call out, "Konk-la-ree!"
The song of the redwing means Spring!

Linda A. Dryfhout

About the Contributor

Linda A. Dryfhout is a poet and children's author. Her poetry has been published in Hello, High Five and Highlights magazines. Anthologies include *What Is A Friend?*; *Things We Eat, Things We Do, Hop To It: Poems To Get You Moving*; *Poetry Friday Anthology for Celebrations* and *Two Truths and A Fib*.

Twitter: @LADryfhout

Website: lindaadryfhout.com

YELLOWSTONE

Moose are roaming in the park.
Wolves are howling after dark.

Bighorn sheep graze on a hill.
Elk calls can sound very shrill.

Bisons' bellows roar like thunder.
Yellowstone is full of wonder!

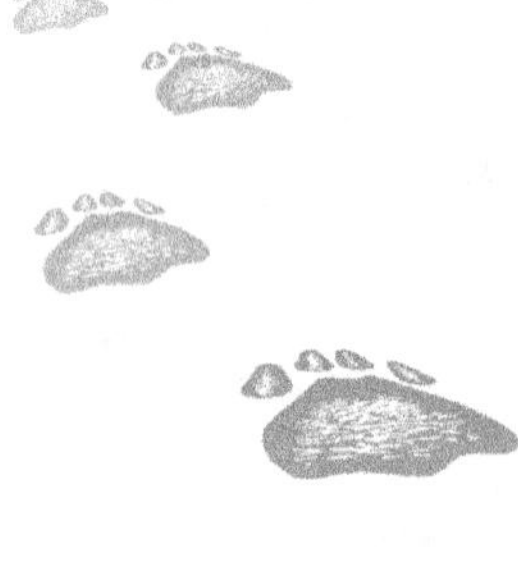

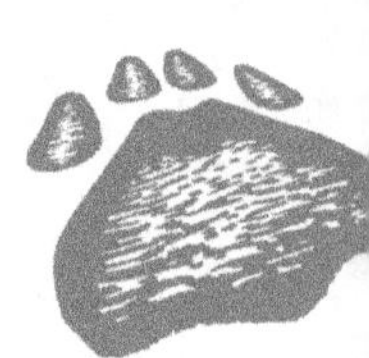

Joan Duris

About the Contributor

Joannie Duris enjoys exploring our world and the world of imagination, never knowing what everyday wonders she might discover right outside her door. She is a children's book author and retired psych nurse. Credits include her first picture book, *B is for Berkshires* (Islandport Press, 2015), and poems in two anthologies from Writers' Loft Press: *Friends & Anemones* (2020) and *Gnomes & UnGnomes* (Nov. 2023).

Joannie grew up in Japan and currently lives in central MA with her two spoiled cats, where she can occasionally be seen chasing black bears away from her birdfeeders. She keeps busy as a Nordic ski patroller, gardening, hiking, bowling, and, of course, writing. A member of SCBWI, 12 x12, and the Writer's Loft, she enjoys writing funny picture books and warly chapter books with quirky, often anthropomorphic characters.

Find out more at www.joanduris.com.

IF TREES COULD TALK

If trees
could talk, would they
whisper like wind on moss,
or rumble greetings, deep and slow?
HELLO-O-O-O.

If trees
could dance, would they
twirl lightly through the woods,
or thump around on gnarly feet?
SWEET.   BEAT.

If trees
could smell, would they
gently sniff hints of spring,
or inhale worlds of sneezy scents?
ACHOO-O-O-O!

TINY TRACKS

Tiny tracks
in fresh snow
tell us tales
of hungry
red squirrels
seeking buried
acorn stashes
as they
d
  a   s
    s   e
      h   l
         c
   i   r
  n   i
      c
    e   s
      n   s
      d l e

SILENT SOUNDS

Hiking in the wilderness,
did you pause, listen to hear
the sounds of scolding squirrels,
the splash of streams polishing rocks,
the gentle whisper of breeze-kissed leaves?

Did you pause, listen to hear
the silent sounds of nature—
flowers tracking sunlight in fields,
water slow-flowing through marshes,
shadows dancing beneath the trees?

Did you hear the silent sounds
of a bobcat watching?

Theresa Gaughan

About the Contributor

Theresa Gaughan has been a classroom teacher for over 25 years, and she currently teaches English/Language Arts and Social Studies to third graders in Knoxville, Tennessee. From the mountains to the beach, Theresa has a deep love and appreciation for all of nature's gifts. She enjoys walking, hiking, bike riding, and kayaking. You can often find her sitting outside to write one of her poems. Her poetry has been published in several anthologies and magazines for children's poetry, including two anthologies edited by Sylvia Vardell and Janet Wong, *What Is a Friend?* and *What is a Family?*

Holding Back the Wild

The grind of machinery shatters the quiet.
Spinning filament relentlessly advances,
guillotining blades of grass and greenery,
replacing untamed wilderness with manicured lawn.

Yet just across the gently flowing creek,
crisscrossed vines tangle among
verdant leaves. Sunlit foliage shades
knobbed knees of hardy trees.
Ferns spread multi-fingered branches,
catching the light with delicate grace.
Yellowed leaves fall to rest on freshly cut grass.

The wild encroaches again.

Summer Rain

With summer heat, it arrives
Tap dancing on rooftops under a blue sky
Painting rainbows on weeping windowpanes
Drumming on sidewalks and streets

Filling hidden hollows
Soaking thirsty soil
Cooling blistering heat
Soothing parched plants

Too soon it departs
Tripping across sunbeams on its way
Sending the promise of another visit
Arcing across the summer sky

In the Mountains / At the Beach

In the mountains,
The air is fresher - high
Amongst the towering trees.
Listening to birdsong,
Face turned upward, I hike
Down a rock-strewn path,
Wildlife skittering out of sight.
Yet I am never as content as when I walk alongside
Sea Turtles nesting nearby.
Sand sifting between toes,
Sunshine bathing bare shoulders,
Listening for the heron's cry,
I meander along the ocean's edge -
The air is salty
At the Beach.

At the Beach
The air is salty
I meander along the ocean's edge -
Listening for the heron's cry
Sunshine bathing bare shoulders
Sand sifting between toes
Sea Turtles nesting nearby
Yet I am never as content as when I walk alongside
Wildlife skittering out of sight
Down a rock-strewn path
Face turned upward, I hike
Listening to birdsong
Amongst the towering trees
The air is fresher - high
In the Mountains

Autumn's Wingless Flock

A breath of wind and WOOSH!
The wingless flock takes flight.
soaring and swooshing over sooty rooftops
swirling cheerfully downward,

looping through pumpkin-spiced air,
lighting on weathered wood fences,
drifting through open doorways,
and decorating patchwork drab yards.

They settle in potato chip piles —
perfect for pets and playgrounds.

Cynthia Greene

About the Contributor

As a child, Cindy Greene wanted to be Shel Silverstein, a kindergarten art teacher, or the president of the World Bank. While not on track for any of those, she loves to write poetry and picture books and make things. Cindy helps non-profits with strategy and metrics, works on issues of racial justice, and spends loads of time with her fun family. She spends much of the day laughing.

Cindy's poetry can be found in several anthologies and stamped in a concrete sidewalk in her town.

Untitled

Forest path beckons.
Slick stones and tangled roots
portend adventure.

Untitled

young fern fronds unfurl
as if slowly stretching from
a long, deep slumber

Kathy Halsey

About the Contributor

Kathy Halsey is a children's author who grew up climbing trees, reading mysteries, and writing poetry in her diary. Her first work-for-hire book, a novelty board book for KiwiCo Press, releases in the fall of 2023. Currently, she serves on the State Library of Ohio's "Choose to Read Ohio" program and writes curricular toolkits for SLO's award-winning children's books. She spends time digging in gardens, writing haiku, and working with her writing group, The Saucy Supremes. Kathy enjoyed careers as a K-12 school librarian, seventh grade English teacher, and bookseller for a children's independent bookstore.

Sunset Serenade

Sun dances. Lingers.
Bows a radiant farewell.
Glowing reviews remain.

Nature Gives and Takes

Jaunty-capped nutkin,
drops by for my daily stroll.
Squirrels spare a new friend.

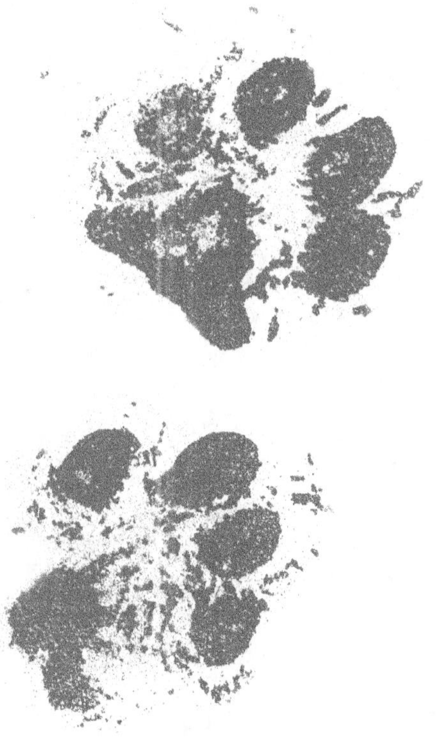

Jon Harris

About the Contributor

Jon Harris was born in Coos Bay, Oregon, and grew up on the Oregon Coast. He started writing poetry in high school and later graduated from North Bend High School. Now, he resides in Portland, Oregon, with his wife Anna, and is currently enrolled at Portland Community College, pursuing studies in creative writing and psychology. Harris has a haiku gallery on Instagram, and his page is called Harris Haiku (@jonharris7717). Hey Hey Books is his first poetry publication.

Summer of Serenity

With the warm sunshine
and serene waterfall sound,
all worries are drowned.

The River

Life is a river
with some chaotic rapids
and some calming streams.

We All Need Connection

Even the lone wolf
will howl to the midnight moon
to find connection.

Loria Harris

About the Contributor

Loria Harris is pursuing her MFA in Creative Writing at Lindenwood University. Her work has been published or is upcoming in *The Mid Rivers Review, The Kings River Review, The Freak, Crimes of the Future,* and *Reverie.* Additionally, she is a recipient of the Jim Haba Poetry Award, the Alyson Dickerman Poetry Prize, the Second Place Achievement in Creative Literature for Phi Theta Kappa's Heartland Region, and the SCC English Student of Promise Award. A lifelong creative, she possesses a Bachelor's Degree in Music Performance, holds two Certificates in Creative Writing from St. Charles Community College, and works as a professional portrait photographer.

Hapiness

Someone always leaves
muddy boots by the door,
he says.

And it's always me,
I realize, a smile
on my face.

I Could Have Crafted a Mansion

I meandered into this life,
stumbling upon it like woods on a sunny day,
cool shade abundant, flickering light to tempt me.
I learned to live on moss, foraged mushrooms,
licking peaty seasoning from my fingers.

Beyond a tinkling stream, there was a banquet
hall—meals, clean water, laughter, but I never saw.
I dwelled among mud and melodies of swallows,
the present need too demanding of my all.
I could have logged the forest, crafted a mansion.

Instead I lived in the library of wild, uncut firs.
Dizzied by the flickers that once tantalized me,
my meandering having led me to enclosure.
I grew immense, uncut fur, swallowed by a cave
that couldn't contain my roar.

The Passing of Time

It's amazing how much time passes without the feeling of it passing while I'm out walking.

I feel gorgeous, one with the earth, who also shows the myriad signs of the passing of time but is not one damn drop less beautiful for it.

I, too, am a mother, have given myself to the trodding of another's feet.

I, too, hold captive the wind, the scent of mildewed earth and broken grass, the warmth of sunshine that hides and peeks, the torrents, the sleet, releasing each when its time is due.

Birdsong and weeds, mating dragonflies tied together like string, trees, prairie, hills nearly too steep, pollen's allergic itch that can never be relieved, all fight for this place, this path carved out amid traffic, shops, the real homes, and garbage truck beeps.

I'm still here.

Look for me.

Jane Heitman Healy

About the Contributor

Jane Heitman Healy is wild about nature and frequently writes about it in her poems and articles for adults and children. She is a retired librarian and teacher who has written three books for teachers and librarians. She lives in South Dakota with her husband and golden retriever and loves spending time with her grandchildren, reading, and meeting fellow writers in person and online.

FOWL WINTER BREAKFAST

pheasants flock
along the frozen roadside
pecking for seed,
picking at pebbles
in the snow,
fluffing their feathers
for warmth,
wary
of danger.

SWEET DREAMS, LAKE CITY

Sun draws the shade over mountains,
Tucks in pines
And kisses peaks goodnight;
Moon follows as arcing nightlight.
With guardian angels twinkling,
Coyotes yip a lullaby.

Valerie Hunter

About the Contributor

Valerie Hunter teaches high school English and has an MFA in writing for children and young adults from Vermont College of Fine Arts. Her stories and poems have appeared in publications including *Sonder, Paper Lanterns, Deep Overstock, Room, Wizards in Space,* and *Capsule Stories,* as well as numerous anthologies. You can find her on Instagram @somanystories_solittletime.

Petals

Each year the dogwood tree
heralds spring's arrival
by arraying itself
in marvelous blooms.
As a rule, Mila isn't a fan of pink,
but these flowers are more than pink—
they're an otherworldly, pearly hue
that never fail to fill her
with a quiet wonder.
She drinks in those petals
at every opportunity, mesmerized
by their delicate perfection.

All too soon, the tree goes back
to its usual self, plain
and ordinary, but Mila still
smiles each time she passes it,
appreciating how this beauty
can go incognito
for the majority of the year
before making its triumphant
return, a reminder
that something unremarkable
still has the potential to blossom
into something glorious.

Lyn Jekowsky

About the Contributor

Writing, from journaling to composing my memoir, has always been a part of who I am. My 36-year practice as a pediatric nurse inspired me to write children's books and poetry, to provide them with tools to journey through life. I participate in a critique group, work with a writing partner, and am an active member of SCBWI, Julie Hedlund's 12x12 Picture Book Challenge, and two other professional writing organizations. As a certified children's yoga instructor, I often base postures and meditations on picture books. When I'm not writing, you can find me at the beach, in my garden, or walking my beloved yellow lab.

TREE UPROOTED

Gnarled yet still rooted,
form patterns on moss.
Swirls of thick anchors
plunge downward then cross.

Form lairs for the wildlife
that romp in the moon.
in curves of pine needles,
sleep all afternoon.

Nature's elegant artwork,
a hidden display,
only seen by the beasts
that meet there to play.

FLICK

He sat upon a lily pad.
He spied a fly.
He flicked his tongue.

He crouched.
He jumped.
He flicked his tongue.

He sprang.
He caught the fly.
He flicked his tongue.

Little Worm

Inching and slinking out of the soil,
feels heat on his belly and needs to recoil.
Exposed and alone, he could become prey,
or squished when he's stepped on
by children at play.

Noticing dirt cracks not too far ahead,
Little Worm wants to squirm home to his bed.
He gathers his courage and takes a deep breath,
wiggles and slithers and writhes one last stretch.

FISH FOR BREAKFAST
(Haiku)

The bunk house door creaks.
It's 4 a. m, Grandpa wakes me
to fish for breakfast.

Launch the old green boat.
We cast out our fishing lines.
A bent rod, a bite.

Creepy whiskered fish,
Grandma will fry for breakfast.
A pat on my back.

Lyn Jekowsky

NAUTILUS
(HAIKU)

Abandoned seashell
Internal chambered spiral
Hermit crab's new home

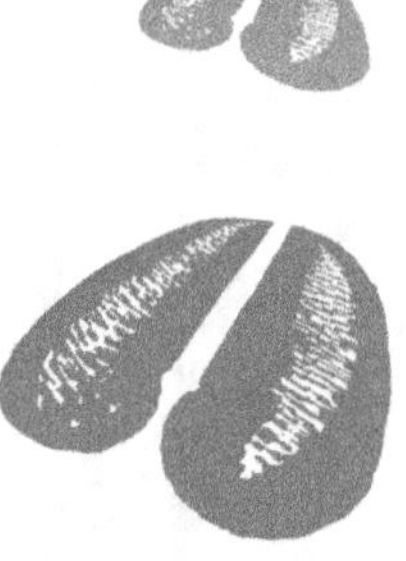

Peter Kaczmarczyk

About the Contributor

Peter Kaczmarczyk was raised in New England and has lived the last 30 years in Southern Indiana. His works are inspired by his life, loves, travels, and experiences. Peter strives to create poems that are without pretense and accessible to all and hopes that his words will resonate with those who read them. He is always surrounded by cats. He has been published in the anthology *Hidden in Childhood* and the *Passionfruit Review* and has poems upcoming in several journals. He is also the co-creator of the Captain Janeway Statue in Bloomington, Indiana.

Face in the Tree

The same place he'd sat
Many times before
Dim light through the window
Usually enough to keep
The predators at bay.
A lone tree stood
Amongst the leaves and dying grass
Thought little grew beneath its canopy.
The air still
A distant animal call all he heard
But this night
Where it had never been before
A face looked out
From the side of the tree.
Part of the bark
No bigger than
The length of his hand
Neither a smile nor a frown
It just stared seriously outward
Slightly toward the ground.
He wondered where
It had been before
And he took joy
That it remained
The next night and all after
He no longer sat alone
No longer just him
With his drink and cigarette
Upon the ancient ground.

Left Behind

The river was old
Once a gathering place
People came to cleanse themselves
Enchanted by its words.
It would charm, was loved
Before it was shrunken
Broken
Forced underground.
Along its banks
You can still find
Bits of lives
People left behind.
The old man rose,
Stumbled away
The river would have
No other visitors today.

Bridget Magee

About the Contributor

Bridget Magee, MFA, TEFL, is an American expat who writes, teaches, and lives in central Switzerland. Bridget's writing has appeared in various publications, both in print *and online, including Chicken Soup for the Soul, Phoenix English Magazine* (EFL), *Smarty Pants Magazine* (audio story), *Whimsical Poet Anthology, Poetry Super Highway*, and many more. She has edited and compiled two poetry anthologies: *10.10 Poetry Anthology and Two Truths and a FIB Poetry Anthology*. She also writes picture books, *Antonio the Meatball* (wee words for wee ones, 2023), and has a Phonics Reading Readiness Workbook series. You can learn more about Bridget and view her poetry blog at bridgetmagee.com

Forest Crawl

I am a grizzly bear,
fishing and foraging in fall.
Preparing to hibernate,
annual forest crawl.

I am gorging on grass.
I am ravaging roots.
I am slurping salmon.
I am feasting on fruits.

I am ingesting insects—
ants, beetles, and winged moths.
I am munching mammals—
elk, mice, but not sloths.

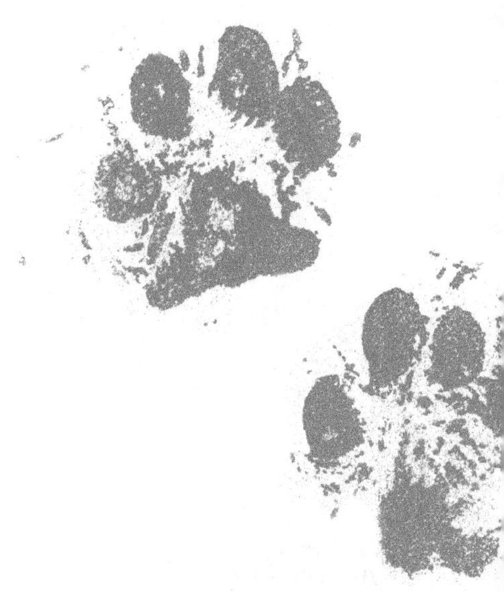

Untitled

winter sun
crocus sprouts
under false pretenses

Untitled

undertones of
urban garden
bluebells

Desert Dwelling

Cactus wrens
make their homes in
Saguaro's finest prickled green
pinstripe suit.

Up in arms,
the cactus declares,
"I'm not a birdhouse!"

Untitled

snow drifts remain
the mudroom weathers
another storm

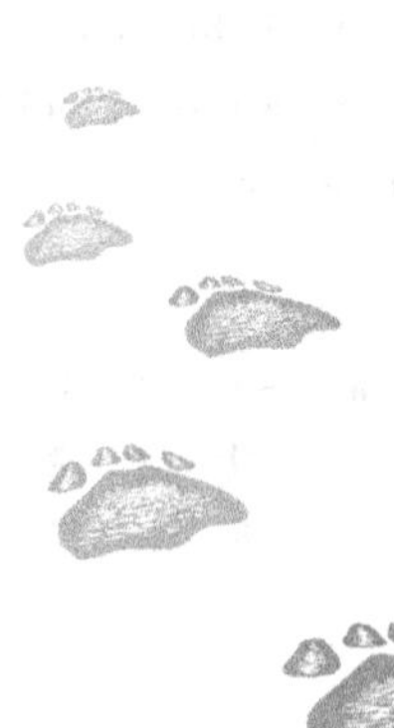

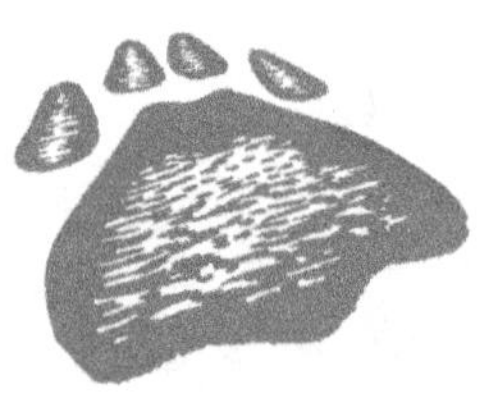

Carmela A. Martino

About the Contributor

Carmela A. Martino is a poet, author, and writing teacher with an MFA in Writing for Children and Young Adults. She has two published novels: *Rosa, Sola* (Candlewick Press), a *Booklist* "Top Ten First Novel for Youth," and *Playing by Heart* (Vinspire Publishing), winner of the Catholic Arts and Letters Award for Children's/YA Fiction. Her poetry for adults and children has appeared in a wide variety of publications, both in print and online. Carmela's writing is often inspired by the natural wonders she observes hiking in the forest preserves near her suburban Chicago home.

For more, see www.carmelamartino.com

Forsythia's Friends

Sparrows sheltering
between yellow buds startle
and take to the sky.

Tulips in Bloom

A vibrant island
of crimson and scarlet floats
on a grass-green sea.

Lilac Time

Spring breezes ruffle
lavender blossoms, sowing
sweet purple perfume.

CLEMATIS

Confident clematis,
keeps watch from her trellis—
a white wooden lattice
eleven feet high.

Whatever the hour,
in sunshine or shower,
her violet flowers
greet all who walk by.

Andy Perrin

About the Contributor

Andy Perrin is a writer/photographer/cyclist/teacher who lives in southern Rhode Island. He often explores the world around him on one of his bikes, and records moments of inspiration in photographs and words. His poetry and photography have been published and are forthcoming in Roi Faineant Press, Full Mood Mag, Green Ink Poetry, Spare Parts Lit, Quibble Literary Journal, Door Is A Jar Magazine, Tiny Wren Lit, and Arboreal Literary Magazine, among others.

Follow his exploration on Twitter @aperrincycling.

The Chipuxet's Flow

I often rest above the
Chipuxet's easy flow

but have never rested
over the same river twice.

The Chipuxet never rests
or looks up at the sky.

It is the sky, the wind,
the rain, the seasons,

the sun, the stars, the first
turned maple leaves

and me.

To The Birds

The bird box simply
grows from the meadow

like all the other things
that grow out there and
seemingly just belong.

That's the perfect spot,
they must think as they
select the family's home.

Just a perfect tree that
grew right there for me
and all those who I love.

The Great Blue Heron

I really wish I could talk
with the great blue heron

so, she would take comfort
in knowing I mean no harm.

Then, she would not fly from
the top of the beaver's dam

and again, from the river bank
high into the blue-gray sky

wings slowly beating into the
horizon never to be seen again.

The Goldfinch

The goldfinch never
wonders of the impact
of what she creates.

She is also unaware
she creates a scene
of absolute wonder.

The Carolina Wren

The winter meadow too
is warm

under autumn's umber
patchwork quilt.

Spring hibernates

until the covers are tossed

and the Carolina wren
returns home
again.

Mark Spuddle

About the Contributor

Mark Spuddle is a former research professor with a PhD in anthropology/archaeology. He is currently a budding children's literature author-illustrator with a penchant for micropoetry and picture books. Dr. Spuddle publishes academically under his real name and reserves his nom de plume for his literary pursuits. He lives with his wife and daughter in the shadow of the Rocky Mountains.

Untitled

deep in my hammock
shallow in my lemonade
rabbit observes me

Untitled

the chill of the wind
seasons the warmth of the sun
I savor the blend

Untitled

drawn to a blossom
whose golden petals hide blue
and hints of scarlet

Untitled

stubborn and icy
spring is denied her debut
winter hogs the stage

Pamela B. Taylor

About the Contributor

Farm life taught Pamela B. Taylor to care for the earth before becoming a teacher and reading specialist. She shared her passion for nature with young students in the classroom. Now, she creates pun-filled tales, poetry and quirky animal adventures. Family vacations to Yellowstone NP, Yosemite NP, Grand Canyon NP and other national parks inspired her to write "Hallowed Spaces," "Mountains," "Sanctuary," and "Our Tents." She is especially excited to have her poems included in WILD. Pamela is pleased to have forthcoming poems featured in FLY, also by Hey Hey Books. She has other poems featured in multiple anthologies by Vardell and Wong and included in a future issue of *Ladybug* Magazine. When she is not writing, she enjoys hiking, reading and crafts. www.pamelabtaylor.com

MOUNTAINS

Multifaceted
Opportunities
Usher
New
Thoughts
About
Intriguing
Natural
Spectacles

OUR TENTS

Our tents
Set up for night
Glow with fluorescent light,
Cocooning us until our dreams
Ignite.

SANCTUARY

The rocks cry out
The waterfall speaks
The canyons echo
The west wind sweeps

Volcanos hiss
The whitecaps roar
The mountains sing
The eagles soar

Wisdom looms
in towering heights
History dwells
in ancient sites

Harmony hovers
in mists and steam
Peace pursues
the mountain stream

Stress evades
and then escapes
in beautiful parks
where all can traipse

HALLOWED SPACES

Big blue sky, open spaces
Set aside, protected places

Hills and mountains, rough terrains
Fertile valleys, flowered plains

Mighty rivers, mountain streams
Glacial bays, vented steams

Scenic arches, cratered lands
Curved bridges, prized badlands

Granite spires, craggy cliffs,
Ancient symbols, petroglyphs

Mangrove swamps, redwood stands
Wild beaches, vast wetlands

Seashores, lakes, waterfalls
Caves, caverns, canyon walls

Watersheds, Great Divide
Woods and forests, petrified

Parched desert, shifting sand
Windswept rocks, thirsty land

Natural fountains, fumaroles,
Lava and caldera bowls

Mist and fog, volcanoes
Thunderclaps, bold rainbows

Bracing air, velvet nights
Starry skies, northern lights

Set aside, protected spaces
Hallowed are these special places

Susan Johnston Taylor

About the Contributor

Susan Johnston Taylor is a Writing Barn fellow and author of Animals in *Surprising Shades: Poems about Earth's Colorful Creatures* (Gnome Road Publishing, March 2023). *School Library Journal* called it "A STEAM-themed poetry collection that should have broad appeal for young readers." Her poetry also appears in *10.10 Poetry Anthology: Celebrating 10 in 10 different ways* and on the Dirigible Balloon. As a freelance writer for over a decade, she's written over a dozen titles for the educational market and published nonfiction articles in children's magazines, including *FACES, Highlights for Children* and *Scout Life*. She lives in Austin, Texas, with her husband and their two rescue dogs.

Untitled

Sunlight warms us as
leaves cast eyelet-lace shadows
on the hiking path.

Untitled

Symphonies of pink
dress the early morning sky
for her overture.

Untitled

Thunder's cymbal crash
yields to rainy lullabies—
like chords resolving.

Joyce Uglow

About the Contributor

Joyce Uglow, poet and picture book author, digs in on topics from bees, trees, and families to rocks, ancient cave art, and fossils trapped in asphalt seeps. She is currently the Co-Chair of SCBWI Wisconsin's Publications Promotions team and additionally sits on the Board of the Wisconsin Center for the Book.

QUEEN OF THE OAK SAVANNA

I am Quercus macrocarpa. My trunk is as bumpy as my life. My crown stretches far and wide. My roots run deep. Some call me Bur Oak Queen.

I sprouted from Squirrel's buried treasure, digging deep, soaking up nature's riches alongside Bluestem and Butterflyweed, growing near Mighty River on the edge of Lush Forest. I felt at home in the company of buffalo and badgers. My pride grew in this First Nations territory where Potawatomi hunted deer and elk in Oak Savanna's sprawling acres.

My leaves and limbs listened to the sun's shine and the wind's whistle. Downy woodpecker's tap-tap-taps and Blue Jays' whisper songs made my heartwood sing. All of nature prepared me for my job as queen. I spread strength with resolute roots mirroring my widening crown.

My trunk expanded ring after ring, one by one, year by year, decade after decade, century after century. Recording stories of scorching hot and freezing cold, streaming sunshine and torrential rains. Stories of cloud-filled days and star-filled nights.

At five rings old, my corky bark saved me from fires. At 35, furry friends nibbled on my first frilly acorns. At 50, I stood one hundred feet strong in this big, bright, and beautiful land. Standing determined, cleaning the air.

But by the time I reached one hundred rings, people from far away began arriving. Exploring. Trading. Building. Pushing their way of life. Erasing. I escaped their axes.

But many of my brother and sister trees did not. At two hundred rings old, oxen and horses plowed around me, locomotives belched smoke over me and into our air. At three hundred rings, tractors buried wildflower meadows. Roads replaced grass. Cars raced by.

But as queen, I stood strong providing homes and shade. I inhaled problems and exhaled solutions. I stayed upright, despite the downsides, despite drought, despite storms of dust sweeping through my branches, blowing across the horizon.

I was tested but did not fall. Day and night. Year after year. Ring after ring after ring.

I stayed.

I am proud to reign in your city park, in the remnants of the once glorious oak savanna. As your queen, I implore you to help me persist, to protect our planet, plant the young, and save the elders.

I, Bur Oak Queen, breathe hope for our planet.

Margarette Wahl

About the Contributor

Margarette Wahl is a Special Education Teacher Aide over twenty years on Long Island. She's a member of Bards Initiative and an Advisor for the Nassau County Poet Laureate Society. She has four chapbooks of poetry with Local Gems Press and published in a number of Anthologies. She wrote her haiku on Wolves after a creative writing class prompt.

Wolf Haiku

Wolf moon way up high
   largest spotlight in the sky
is it night or day

Howling overheard
   wolf cries in the distance
nature's wild song

Small pups crying out
  tiny howls for their mom
wolf sanctuary

Underneath moonlight
  wolves howl with their heads
up to a star-filled sky

119

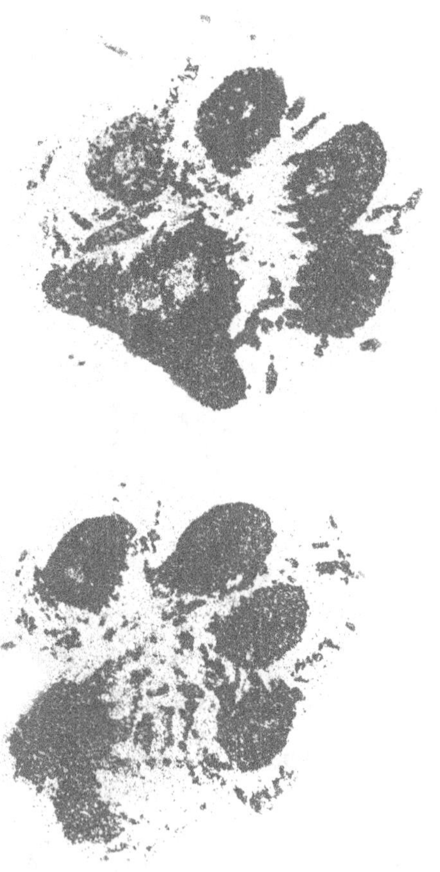

Contest Winners

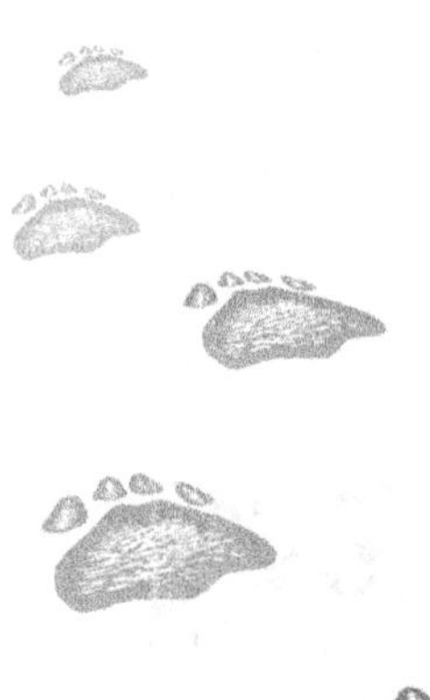

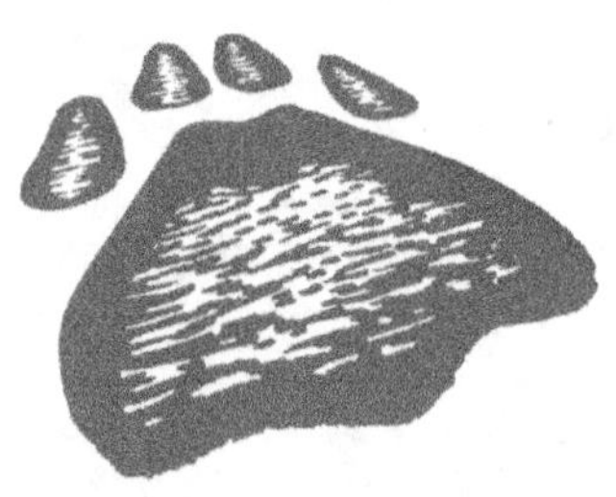

Tara Boyles

About the Contributor

Taya Boyles is a writer based in Richmond, Virginia. She is currently a senior pursuing a Bachelor of Arts in English at Virginia Commonwealth University. Taya's writing journey started at just eight years old, and she has come a long way from misspelling glue. Since then, her poetry and flash fiction have appeared in literary magazines such as Split Lip Magazine, Vermillion, Pwatem, Hot Pot Magazine, Radical Zine, and more.

The National Park

Nature is a permanent institution
with government and a state address
that blooms in the off-season months
while winterized humans fall to
seasonal depression
into a
sinkhole that we bury and birth life on.

The inter-dimensional floating
temples resist the gravitational
pull of space and time and National Parks
have earned past just their enshrinement.

Oh, poor solipsist,
go and hug a tree.

Tell me you don't feel the roots humming
see the blue in the wind and
bear the weight of the beating heart
of an injured Robin who only
knows your palms.

Joan Duris

About the Contributor

Joannie Duris enjoys exploring our world and the world of imagination, never knowing what everyday wonders she might discover right outside her door. She is a children's book author and retired psych nurse. Credits include her first picture book, *B is for Berkshires* (Islandport Press, 2015), and poems in two anthologies from Writers' Loft Press: *Friends & Anemones* (2020), and *Gnomes & UnGnomes* (Nov. 2023).

Joannie grew up in Japan and currently lives in central MA with her two spoiled cats, where she can occasianly be seen chasing black bears away from her bird feeds. She keeps busy as a Nordic ski patroller, gardening, hiking, bowling, and of course, writing. A member of SCBWI, 12 x 12, and the Writer's Loft, she enjoys writing funny picture books and early chapter books with quirky, often anthropomorphic characters. Find out more at www.joanduris.com.

The Camper

Perched on a rock
tent at my back
I silently watch
as
morning mist
fades
into day.

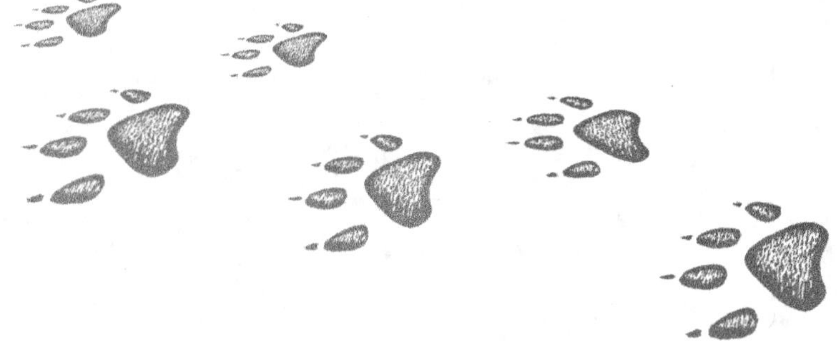

Miriam Wade

About the Contributor

Miriam Wade is a Minnesota local who writes young adult fantasy, adventure, and urban fantasy driven by resilient young women, filled with twisty plots, and garnished with a hint of romance. She loves coffee, playing video games, and riding her bicycle. When she is not writing, she enjoys spending time with her husband, their two young daughters, and their cat. Wade is the author of the award-winning steampunk Arthurian inspired series, *One Sword Saga*, and the forthcoming paranormal urban fantasy, *The Woman of Blythe Manor*, as well as a featured poet in several anthologies.

Instagram: www.instagram.com/miriam.wade.author
Facebook: www.facebook.com/miriam.wade.author
Twitter: www.twitter.com/wade_author
TikTok: www.tiktok.com/@miriam.wade.author
Website: www.miriam-wade.com

Untitled

Wilderness beckons, to break free,
In the midst of chaos, a place to be.
Living life unchained, with untamed glee,
Dancing with nature, in pure harmony.

Animal Tracks Tapestry

In forests deep, where secrets dwell,
Where nature weaves its mystic spell,
Animals tread upon the earth's own page,
Leaving imprints, age after age.

The mighty lion, with paws of grace,
Leaves his mark in a regal embrace,
His fierce presence, commanding and grand,
Imprinted in the shifting sand.

The agile deer, swift and light,
Leaps through meadows, taking flight,
Leaving behind a delicate trace,
A dance of elegance, full of grace.

The bear, with heavy steps and might,
Strolls through forests, day and night,
Leaving tracks that speak of strength,
Of wilderness, and its endless length.

The fox, a cunning trickster, sly,
Leaves tracks that whisper, passing by,
A clever tale of wits and guile,
Unraveling secrets mile by mile.

The owl, in silence, takes flight,
Leaving no trace within the night,
But in the snow, its feathers glide,
An intricate pattern, where stories hide.

And so, the animal tracks unfold,
A symphony of stories yet untold,
In every print, a world awakes,
A tapestry of life that nature makes.

Acknowledgements

Thank you Marcie Flinchum Atkins, Benjamin Bishop, Taya Boyles, Candice Marley Conner, Patricia Cooley, Linda M. Crate, Robert Daniel, Leslie Degnan, Linda A. Dryfhout, Joan Duris, Theresa Gaugh, Cynthia Greene, Kathy Halsey, Jon Harris, Loria Harris, Jan Heitman Healy, Valerie Hunter, Lyn Jekowsky, Peter Kaczmarczyk, Bridget Magee, Carmela A. Martino, Andy Perrin, Mark Spuddle, Pamela B. Taylor, Susan Johnston Taylor, Joyce P. Uglow, Miriam Wade, and Margarette Wahl for your generous contributions and showcasing your poetry in *Wild*.

Thank you also Jeanette Barroso (cover designer), Elise Pullen (illustrator), and Alyssa Myers (editor) for giving your time and dedication.

Thank you, reader, for your investment and for reading the exceptional work presented to you in this anthology.

Interested in further supporting wildlife? Please consider visiting:

nwf.org

defenders.org

wildlandsconservancy.org

audubon.org

Finally, we thank the wildlife, especially those mentioned within this book, for inspiring these poems. What would our country look like without these animals and plants? We hope that future generations will never have to find out.

A portion of the proceeds will be donated to help support wildlife.